THE NEW YORK JETS

BY JANIE SCHEFFER

NFL TEAM PROFILES

EPIC

BELLWETHER MEDIA ★ MINNEAPOLIS, MN

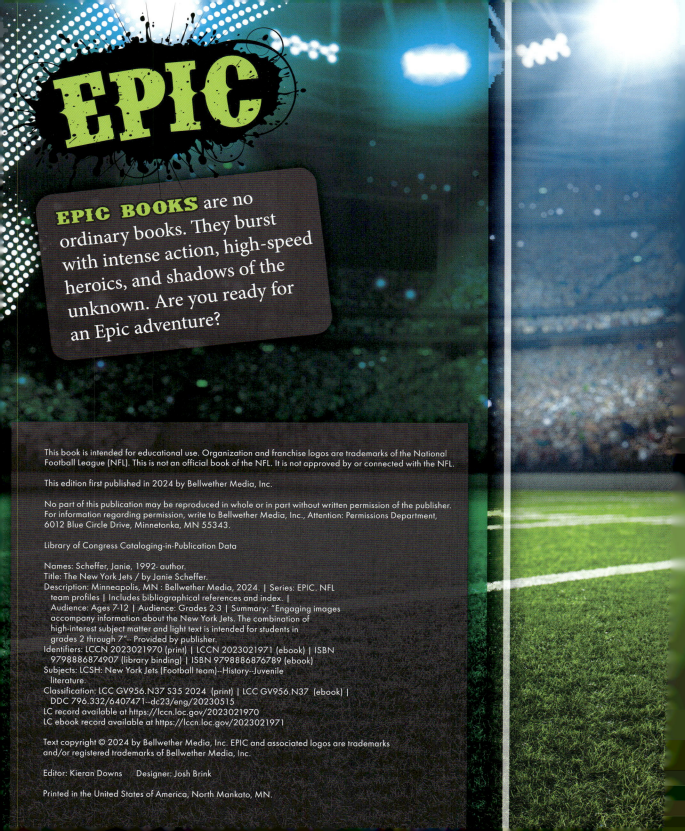

EPIC

EPIC BOOKS are no ordinary books. They burst with intense action, high-speed heroics, and shadows of the unknown. Are you ready for an Epic adventure?

This book is intended for educational use. Organization and franchise logos are trademarks of the National Football League (NFL). This is not an official book of the NFL. It is not approved by or connected with the NFL.

This edition first published in 2024 by Bellwether Media, Inc.

No part of this publication may be reproduced in whole or in part without written permission of the publisher. For information regarding permission, write to Bellwether Media, Inc., Attention: Permissions Department, 6012 Blue Circle Drive, Minnetonka, MN 55343.

Library of Congress Cataloging-in-Publication Data

Names: Scheffer, Janie, 1992- author.
Title: The New York Jets / by Janie Scheffer.
Description: Minneapolis, MN : Bellwether Media, 2024. | Series: EPIC. NFL team profiles | Includes bibliographical references and index. | Audience: Ages 7-12 | Audience: Grades 2-3 | Summary: "Engaging images accompany information about the New York Jets. The combination of high-interest subject matter and light text is intended for students in grades 2 through 7"-- Provided by publisher.
Identifiers: LCCN 2023021970 (print) | LCCN 2023021971 (ebook) | ISBN 9798886874907 (library binding) | ISBN 9798886876789 (ebook)
Subjects: LCSH: New York Jets (Football team)--History--Juvenile literature.
Classification: LCC GV956.N37 S35 2024 (print) | LCC GV956.N37 (ebook) | DDC 796.332/6407471--dc23/eng/20230515
LC record available at https://lccn.loc.gov/2023021970
LC ebook record available at https://lccn.loc.gov/2023021971

Text copyright © 2024 by Bellwether Media, Inc. EPIC and associated logos are trademarks and/or registered trademarks of Bellwether Media, Inc.

Editor: Kieran Downs   Designer: Josh Brink

Printed in the United States of America, North Mankato, MN.

TABLE OF CONTENTS

A LONG RUN	4
THE HISTORY OF THE JETS	6
THE JETS TODAY	14
GAME DAY!	16
NEW YORK JETS FACTS	20
GLOSSARY	22
TO LEARN MORE	23
INDEX	24

A LONG RUN

In 2022, the Jets lead the Packers 17–10. It is the beginning of the fourth quarter.

Jets **running back** Breece Hall gets the ball. He runs for a 34-yard **touchdown**. The Jets go on to win the game 27–10!

BREECE HALL

THE HISTORY OF THE JETS

The Jets began in 1960. They were first called the New York Titans. They played in the American Football League (AFL).

In 1963, they became the Jets. Two years later, Joe Namath became **quarterback**. He helped the team to many wins!

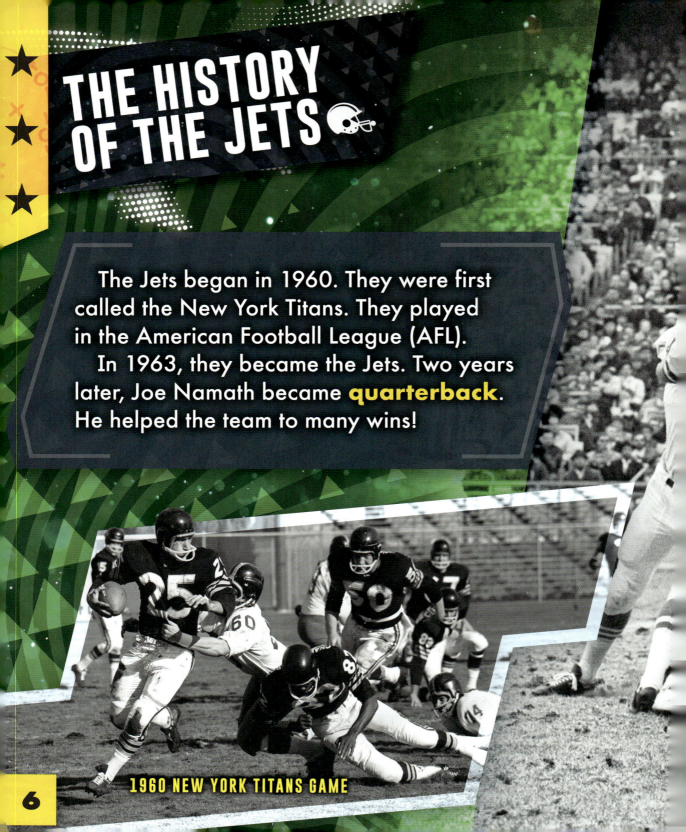

1960 NEW YORK TITANS GAME

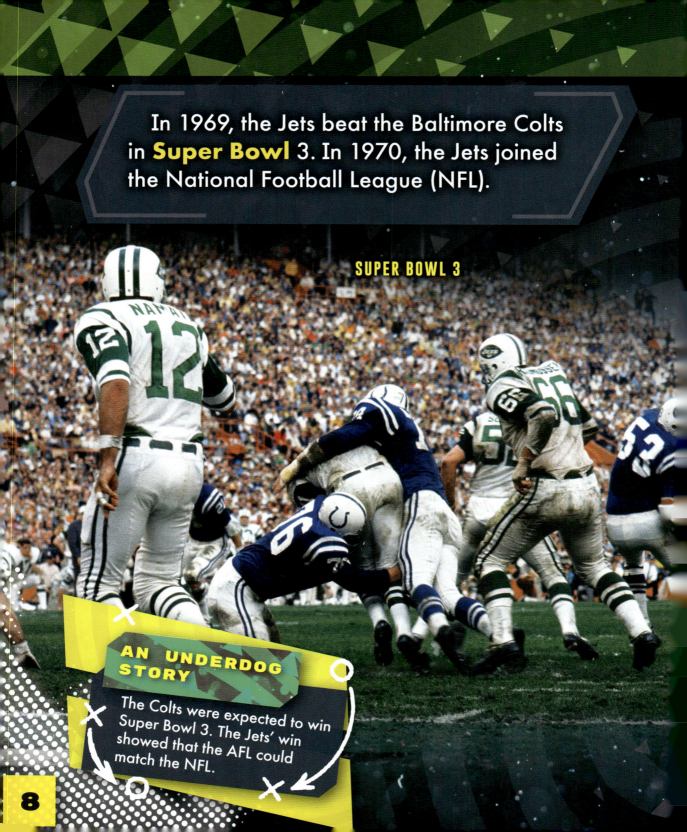

In 1969, the Jets beat the Baltimore Colts in **Super Bowl** 3. In 1970, the Jets joined the National Football League (NFL).

SUPER BOWL 3

AN UNDERDOG STORY

The Colts were expected to win Super Bowl 3. The Jets' win showed that the AFL could match the NFL.

1984 JETS GAME

The Jets did not make the **playoffs** in the 1970s. In the 1980s, they had little playoff success.

The Jets struggled again in the early 1990s. But in 1998, the Jets won their **division**.

1998 PLAYOFF GAME

Running back Curtis Martin was a key player. He helped the Jets find some success in the early 2000s.

LATER TO THE GAME

Curtis Martin started playing football later than most. He began playing during his senior year of high school.

CURTIS MARTIN

The Jets played well in the 2009 and 2010 seasons. Each season they made it to the AFC **Championship** Game. But they lost both times.

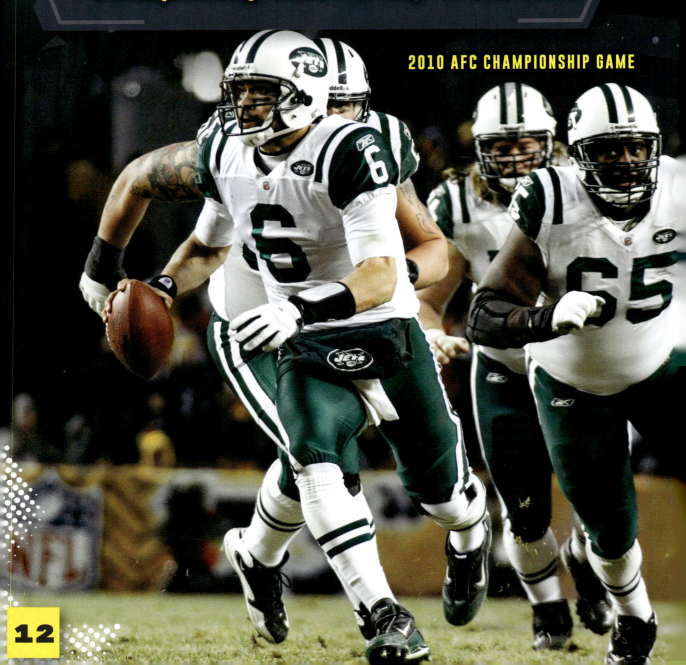

2010 AFC CHAMPIONSHIP GAME

The Jets failed to make the playoffs from 2011 to 2022. They hope for more success in the future.

TROPHY CASE

PLAYOFF appearances: 14

AFC EAST championships: 2

SUPER BOWL championships: 1

AFL championships: 1

THE JETS TODAY

JETS VS. PATRIOTS

The Jets play home games at MetLife **Stadium**. It is located in East Rutherford, New Jersey.

The Jets play in the AFC East division. Their biggest **rival** is the New England Patriots.

SHARED HOME

The Jets share their home field with the New York Giants.

LOCATION

MetLife Stadium
East Rutherford, New Jersey

NEW JERSEY

15

GAME DAY!

Jets fans wear green and cheer loudly. "J-E-T-S! Jets! Jets! Jets!" is the most popular cheer.

In 2013, the Aviators **Drumline** started supporting the team. They perform before and during games.

AVIATORS DRUMLINE

Before each home game, an air raid siren sounds. A fan or celebrity is picked to sound it. Jets fans call themselves "Gang Green." For over 60 years, fans have cheered for the Jets!

AIR RAID SIREN

★ FAMOUS PLAYERS ★

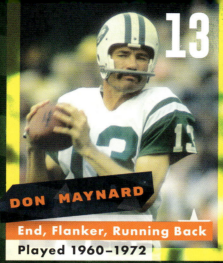

13

DON MAYNARD

End, Flanker, Running Back
Played 1960–1972

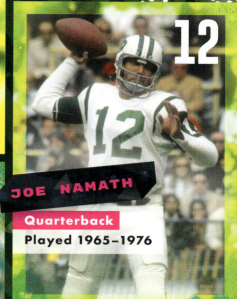

12

JOE NAMATH

Quarterback
Played 1965–1976

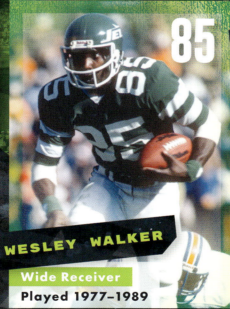

85

WESLEY WALKER

Wide Receiver
Played 1977–1989

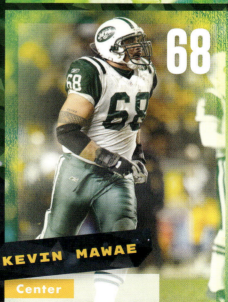

68

KEVIN MAWAE

Center
Played 1998–2005

24

DARRELLE REVIS

Cornerback
Played 2007–2012, 2015–2016

19

NEW YORK JETS FACTS

LOGO

JOINED THE NFL	1970 (AFL 1960-1969)
NICKNAME	Gang Green

MASCOT NONE

CONFERENCE American Football Conference (AFC)

COLORS

DIVISION AFC East

 Buffalo Bills
 Miami Dolphins
 New England Patriots

STADIUM

★ MetLife Stadium ★

opened April 10, 2010

holds **82,500** people

TIMELINE

1960 — The Jets begin as the New York Titans

1963 — The team is renamed the New York Jets

1969 — The Jets win Super Bowl 3

1998 — The Jets win their division

2011 — The Jets play in the AFC Championship Game

RECORDS

All-Time Passing Leader
Joe Namath
27,057 yards

All-Time Rushing Leader
Curtis Martin
10,302 yards

All-Time Receiving Leader
Don Maynard
11,732 yards

All-Time Scoring Leader
Pat Leahy
1,470 points

GLOSSARY

championship—a contest to decide the best team or person

division—a group of NFL teams from the same area that often play against each other; there are eight divisions in the NFL.

drumline—a group of musicians who play drums and cymbals, usually to pump up a crowd

playoffs—games played after the regular season is over; playoff games determine which teams play in the championship game.

quarterback—a player whose main job is to throw and hand off the ball

rival—a long-standing opponent

running back—a player whose main job is to run with the ball

stadium—an arena where sports are played

Super Bowl—the annual championship game of the NFL

touchdown—a score that occurs when a team crosses into their opponent's end zone with the football; a touchdown is worth six points.

TO LEARN MORE

AT THE LIBRARY

Abdo, Kenny. *New York Jets*. Minneapolis, Minn.: Abdo Zoom, 2022.

Coleman, Ted. *New York Jets All-time Greats*. Mendota Heights, Minn.: Press Box Books, 2022.

Whiting, Jim. *The Story of the New York Jets*. Mankato, Minn.: The Creative Company, 2020.

ON THE WEB

FACTSURFER

Factsurfer.com gives you a safe, fun way to find more information.

1. Go to www.factsurfer.com.

2. Enter "New York Jets" into the search box and click 🔍.

3. Select your book cover to see a list of related content.

INDEX

AFC Championship Game, 12
AFC East, 10, 15, 20
air raid siren, 18
American Football League (AFL), 6, 8, 20
Aviators Drumline, 16
cheer, 16
colors, 16, 20
East Rutherford, New Jersey, 14, 15
famous players, 19
fans, 16, 18
Hall, Breece, 5
history, 4, 5, 6, 8, 9, 10, 11, 12, 13, 16

Martin, Curtis, 11
MetLife Stadium, 14, 15, 17, 20
Namath, Joe, 6, 7
name, 6
National Football League (NFL), 8, 20
New York Jets facts, 20-21
playoffs, 9, 10, 13
positions, 5, 6, 11
records, 21
rival, 15
Super Bowl, 8
timeline, 21
trophy case, 13

The images in this book are reproduced through the courtesy of: Margaret Bowles/ AP Images, cover (hero); George Wirt, cover (stadium); All-Pro Reels/ Wikipedia, p. 3; Stacy Revere/ Getty, pp. 4, 5; Bob Campbell/ AP Images, pp. 6, 21 (1960); Bettmann/ Getty, pp. 6-7, 21 (1963); Focus On Sport/ Getty, pp. 8-9, 19 (Don Maynard, Joe Namath, Wesley Walker), 21 (1969), 21 (1969, Don Maynard) Evan Pinkus/ AP Images, p. 10; G. Newman Lowrance/ AP Images, pp. 10-11; Gene J. Puskar/ AP Images, pp. 12-13; UPI/ Alamy, p. 14; NFL/ Wikipedia, p. 15 (Jets logo), 20 (Jets logo, Bills logo, Dolphins logo, Patriots logo, AFC logo); ZUMA Press/ Alamy, p. 15; Robin Marchant/ Getty, p. 16; Tim Clayton/ Getty, pp. 16-17; Al Pereira/ Getty, pp. 18-19; Tomasso DeRosa/ AP Images, p. 19 (Kevin Mawae); Icon Sportswire/ Getty, p. 19 (Darrelle Revis); REUTERS, p. 20 (fans); Fotos593/ AP Images, p. 20 (stadium); Mitchell B. Reibel/ AP Images, p. 21 (1998); Nick Laham/ Getty, p. 21 (2011); Tony Tomsic, p. 21 (Joe Namath, Pat Leahy); Paul Spinelli, p. 23.